Praise for
Savor the Savior

Kristin has always inspired and deepened my faith through her writing and gift of storytelling. In *Savor the Savior*, Kristin perfectly captures how to draw near to Him during the Christmas season. We have all experienced the busyness of the holidays overshadowing Christ's birth, and Savor the Savior is a simple yet powerful journey through the Advent season that refocuses our heart and mind on celebrating our Lord.

—James Gleghorn
Vice President, Tim Tebow Foundation

I own and have read many devotionals, and I have written a devotional. But I have not yet come across a devotional like the one you are holding in your hands. The Christmas season can be one of the most time-consuming seasons of the year, and although the focus of the season is Christ, we often spend more time focusing on gifts, our families, and Christmas programs than we do feeding our soul with the very essence of the holiday. Kristin Saatzer has masterfully brought it all back into focus for us with Savor the Savior. You will find the individual devotions are short and full, I mean full of goodness. The devos are rich with history, prayers, information, relatability, and something hearty for the reader to meditate on. The book will leave you wanting more—it's that good! You will be tempted to turn the page, and turn the page, and turn the page again, forgetting that it is indeed a daily devotional. Enjoy!

—Brandie Manigault
Author of *New Day Fresh Start*
Cofounder of Healing Voice Ministries

i

Like most people seeking to elevate the holidays from commercial compromising and hectic hustle, every Christmas I look for fresh perspectives and insights on the timeless narrative of the incarnation. In this devotional, Kristin Saatzer has given us such a gift. In quick daily doses, she helps us rise above the clutter and clamor by captivating our imagination and imparting hope to our hearts by elucidating the names and attributes of the God who became man. Her family reflections and practical counsel have helped me over and again find my heart's true home in a season when I need it most.

—Mike Johnson
Chaplain and Dean of Student Life, Linfield Christian School

SAVOR
the
SAVIOR

Twenty-Five Devotions
for Advent and Christmas
Inspired by the Names of Jesus

SAVOR
the
SAVIOR

Twenty-Five Devotions
for Advent and Christmas
Inspired by the Names of Jesus

Kristin Saatzer

REDEMPTION
PRESS

I dedicate this book to you, Mom, my biggest fan.
My devotion to Jesus and Christmas began in your
arms.
I love you.

Contents

But when the fullness of the time was come, God sent forth His son,

made of a woman, made under the law.

—Galatians 4:4 KJV

The central message asserted by Christmas is the Incarnation.

They say that God became Man…

If this thing happened, it was the central event in the history of earth.

—C. S. Lewis, Miracles

Preface

If there's a book that you want to read, but it hasn't been
written yet, then you must write it.
—Toni Morrison

Dear Reader,

For years I looked, and for years I waited for a book like the
one you hold in your hands: a Christmas writing that captures
the essence of the names of the Savior. A book that provides daily
readings that are biblically deep, reflective, and yes, *quick*. Many an
Advent season came and went as I talked myself into and then
out of writing. With fearful thoughts, like *Who am I to handle this
task? The word of God is serious business*, and *I am no theologian*, I
brought the matter to God.

After an "aha!" moment in prayer, this non-theologian began the
journey of writing her first book. I feel as if I had a crash course in
Bible school after countless hours of research and study. My passion
for and knowledge of God and His word enlarged and fortified. He
climbed each step with me in this writing expedition. Here I stand,
breathless and grateful on the other side of the mountain. Still, I am
no theologian. Just a gal loved and led by a gracious God. This is my
small offering to Him.

My prayer for you, dear reader, is that you will infuse your
holiday season with the gift of Jesus each day and grow in love,
knowledge, and intimacy with your Savior. Reflect with depth; use
a notebook, journal, or the space provided to answer questions and
write your prayers, thoughts, and thanks to God.

Before we begin our journey together, let us hit a few points in
preparation. This is Christmas: God became a man, His glory visible
in a new form (see Hebrews 1:3). Prophets long predicted this event,
and the coming of Christ confirmed the promises of God, fulfilling
prophecies. The Old Testament prophets gave many names to the
Savior. In this book, you will read of prophetically given names
and meanings. We will cover titles granted by the angels, John the

Baptist, New Testament writers, as well as some of the names Jesus called Himself.

It might be helpful for us to look at the meaning of the word *Advent*:

ADVENT (noun): A coming; appropriately, the coming of our Savior, and in the calendar . . . it is intended as a season of devotion, with reference to the coming of Christ in the flesh, and his second coming to judge the world. —*Webster's 1828 Dictionary* online

I love how *Webster's* puts it: "intended as a season of devotion." May this book, a devotional, be a tool in this season. Give yourself a gift this Christmas —the gift of some quiet time of the soul, devoted to savoring your Savior.

Merry Christmas!
Blessings,
Kristin

December 1
Alpha and Omega

I am the Alpha and the Omega, the First and the Last
(the Before all and the End of all).
—Revelation 22:13 AMP

Alpha and Omega are the first and last letters of the Greek
alphabet, and a title of Christ and God in the Book of
Revelation. —*Wikipedia.org*

Imagine the triumphant scene: Christ standing among seven golden lampstands, clothed in a long robe, white hair, eyes blazing like fire, with bronzed and glowing feet. Jesus Christ is the star of the dazzling play called *The Book of Revelation*, as written by John.

Who is this Jesus? We find Him throughout the Bible, from the beginning of Genesis to the end of Revelation. God incarnate. A perfect place to begin our Advent journey together is to start at the *end* of the Bible. Our Jesus, the beginning of all things, and the One who promises to return for the dramatic finale.

He is the A to Z, the sum of the Scriptures and everything in between:

Christ is the central figure of the Old and New Testament. " In the beginning was the Word, and the Word was with God, and the Word was God" (John 1:1). "The Word became flesh and made his dwelling among us" (John 1:14).

Christ culminates the end of the law. "Do not think that I have come to abolish the Law or the Prophets; I have not come to abolish them but to fulfill them" (Matthew 5:17).

Christ initiates and completes our journey with Him. "Looking unto Jesus the author and finisher of our faith; who for the joy that was set before him endured the cross, despising the shame, and is set down at the right hand of the throne of God" (Hebrews 12:2 KJV).

As you breathe in this fresh first day of December, remember the star of this Christmas show. He is the opening act and the closing scene: Our Jesus, our Alpha and Omega. May He be your First and Last and everything in between this Christmas season.

Reflection

1. As you begin Advent, where do you need God to take over as the Author of your faith? The Author of your time? The Author of your finances?

2. Commit to beginning and ending each Advent day with Jesus. Give Him the first and the last of your day.

Prayer

Dear Alpha and Omega, You are the entirety of the Scriptures. I want to focus on You this season, as I never have before. So today, I claim You as my Alpha and Omega, the Beginning and the End. My God incarnate.

Amen

Unto Us a Boy Is Born

Fifteenth Century Latin Hymn for Christmas
[Verses 4 and 5]

Now may Mary's Son, who came

So long ago to love us,

Lead us all with hearts aflame

Unto the joys above us.

Omega and Alpha He!

Let the organ thunder,

While the choir with peals of glee

Doth rend the air asunder.

December 2
Redeemer

Praise the Lord, the God of Israel, because he has visited
and redeemed his people. He has sent us a mighty Savior
from the royal line of his servant David, just as he promised
through his holy prophets long ago.
—Luke 1:68–70 NLT

The Redeemer will come.
—Isaiah 59:20

Redeemer (noun):
1. One who redeems or ransoms.
2. The Savior of the world, Jesus Christ.
—*Webster's 1828 Dictionary* online

Have you ever had the feeling of watching yourself from above, observing a scene that seemed surreal?

One (okay, maybe more than one) of these "spells" or "tizzy fits" occurred in the middle of the Christmas season years ago. Me, a spinning top, ready to lose steam and hit the wall. My life, overfull: boys with the stomach flu, a Christmas-tree-climbing toddler, a big messy dog in her chewing phase, and me suffering from a strained relationship. I was also over-budgeted, and over-scheduled. Hit the wall, I did. It was dreadful, folks: mom, in the middle of the living room kicking her feet, flailing her arms, with sounds like dolphin shrieks sputtering from her mouth. My poor family.

Later, after the therapists left (Ha!) and I begged forgiveness from my people, I got away alone. I asked the Savior to save my season. I begged the Lord to redeem my heart. To redeem my family. Our

Redeemer came for times like these. Our Redeemer makes us whole.

Thankfully, I learned from that ugly experience. Nowadays, before I wrap the first gift or bake the first batch of goodies, I take intentional time for the following:

1. I focus on the Redeemer. I read Scripture as I ponder the miracle of my redeemed soul.

2. I pray over my calendar and budget. To the best of my ability, I plan and schedule the holiday giving and expenses. I commit these to God, and I pray that I will please Him with my time and treasures and that I may find peace, strength, and wisdom in Him.

3. I pray for peace in my relationships, and that the Lord will show me when and where I need to make amends.

How amazing it is that our merciful Redeemer joins us in our messes, and our tizzy fits. Let us look to Him *first* as we fill our calendars and holiday moments.

Reflection

1. Take time alone with the Redeemer to plan and redeem your holiday season.

2. Read: Romans 3:24; Ephesians 1:7; and Colossians 1:14. Journal the truths you find and thank Him for them.

Prayer

Dear Redeemer, thank You for redeeming our souls by Your birth, death, and resurrection. You alone can redeem our hearts, our season, and our relationships. We ask You to do so today and each day of Advent.

Amen

Oh Thou Joyful Day

Traditional German
Anonymous, Eighteenth Century
[Verse 2]

O thou joyful day, O thou blessed day,

Holy peaceful Christmastide!

Christ's light is beaming, our souls redeeming,

Laud Him, O laud Him on every side!

December 3
Wonderful Counselor

He is wonderful in counsel
—Isaiah 28:29 ESV

And His name shall be called Wonderful Counselor
—Isaiah 9:6 KJV

Counselor (noun): One who gives advice or help. Sometimes
the Bible uses the word *Counselor* as another name for Jesus.
In the New Testament, the Holy Spirit is also called "Counselor
of Christians." —*What the Bible Is All About*

It might not be *A Wonderful Life* for you this Advent, or *The Most Wonderful Time of the Year*.

The holidays bring on a cocktail of complicated emotions for many of us. This may be the first Christmas after a divorce. A trauma. A loss. Bankruptcy. A health crisis. Does the holiday season trigger terrible memories? Perhaps beautiful memories of happy times past? Are you lonely? Some of us face Christmas chaos.

Is your heart distressed? Your body exhausted? Your soul depleted?

Are you on a roller coaster—up one minute, down the next?

A few years ago, as Christmas approached, dread filled my heart. I faced feuding family members, and painful memories triggered sorrow. I waded through financial yuck and physical trials. Not so wonderful. I wanted to fall asleep and wake up after January 1.

Yet, I knew to turn to my Wonderful Counselor. I opened His word and rested with Him in prayer, pouring out the pain of my heart.

Mindfulness is essential as we advance through Advent, no matter what our circumstances. So as I sat, I forged a plan of action for self-care and soul-care. I encourage you to ponder the following:

- Anticipate sadness and make daily space for grief
- Make sure your calendar provides down and rest time
- Plan activities that bring you joy (A funny movie? A walk with a friend?)
- Take time with your Wonderful Counselor for daily prayer and Scripture reading
- Anticipate triggers and conditions that may cause pain
- Talk with others about your struggles and enlist prayer
- See a therapist or join a support group (check your church for a group or find a Celebrate Recovery near you: celebraterecovery.com).

Precious friend, God knows your pain. He is wonderful in counsel. He will never leave you. Your Counselor loves you beyond measure. I encourage you to seek support and self-care.

Reflection

1. Create your own plan for self-care and soul-care for the season.

2. Read: Jeremiah 32:19, Proverbs 8:14 and Romans 11:33

Prayer

Dear Wonderful Counselor, I give You my emotions. I invite You in as my Counselor and companion. I lay my struggles and joys before You as I anticipate all that the holidays may encompass.
Amen

Wonderful Counselor

Negro Spiritual
Anonymous, Nineteenth Century
[Verse 1]

Oh, who do you call the wonderful counselor?

Oh, glory hallelujah!

Oh, glory hallelujah!

Glory hallelujah to the newborn king!

[Verse 2]

Oh, I call Jesus the wonderful counselor.

Oh, glory hallelujah!

Oh, glory hallelujah!

Glory hallelujah to the newborn king!

December 4
Dayspring

You do well if you pay attention to this as you would to a
light shining in a murky place, until the day dawns and the
morning star rises in your hearts.
—2 Peter 1:19 NET

Through the tender mercy of our God; whereby the dayspring from on high has visited us, to give light to them
that sit in darkness and in the shadow of death,
to guide our feet in the way of peace.
—Luke 1:78–79 KJV

Dayspring (noun): The dawn; the beginning of the day,
or first appearance of light. —*Webster's 1828 Dictionary* online

Are you a fan of the morning? It has taken me years to get here, but
I cherish it now. It did not come naturally. Even as a child I was a
grumpy slow starter. I am a nine-to-nine person, capable of intelligi-
ble conversation only between those hours (and that is
debatable). These days, though, I cherish my early morning time
spent in prayer and Bible reading and savoring the sunrise
showing off beyond the tall trees. The day, fresh and sparkling,
ripe for the taking.

God's Word is full of beautiful light imagery and the picture of
Christ as a sunrise. A pastor's resource called *The Pulpit Commentary*
explains:

"In his temple service at Jerusalem the priest must have seen
the ruddy dawn rise grandly over the dark chain of the distant
mountains, and lighting up with a blaze of golden glory the
everlasting hills as they stood round about Jerusalem. The
thought which pictured the advent of the Messiah as a sunrise was

a favorite one with the prophets."

The prophet Isaiah uses the metaphor of Christ as a sunrise in chapter 60, verse 1 (NLT). It says, "For the glory of the Lord rises to shine on you." As does Malachi in chapter 4 verse 2 (KJV): "But unto you that fear my Name shall the Sun of Righteousness arise with healing in his wings."

Jerusalem needed a sunrise, a Dayspring to dawn upon their austere blackness. This Dayspring *will* come a second and final time, according to the Bible. May we pay attention to His light as we live and wait for His coming. May we shine for Him as His children of light. Until the time of His return, we find Him in the beauty of the sunrise—as our day dawns, and we focus our thoughts on Him.

Reflection

1. Who is this Dayspring? Why did He need to come to this dark world?

2. Set your intention on beginning your Advent mornings with Jesus. Invite Him to rise in your heart as you rise from your bed.

Prayer

Dear Dayspring, fill my Christmas mornings with Your Savior-sunrise. I commit to seeking You first as I rise each day this season.
Amen

O Come, O Come, Emmanuel

Latin, Ninth Century
Translated by John M. Neale, 1851
[Verses 4 and 5]

Oh come, Thou Dayspring, come and cheer

Our spirits by Thine advent here;

Disperse the gloomy clouds of night,

And death's dark shadows put to flight.

O come, O Bright and Morning Star,

and bring us comfort from afar!

Dispel the shadows of the night

and turn our darkness into light.

[Refrain]

Rejoice! Rejoice! Immanuel

shall come to you, O Israel.

December 5
Bread of Life

Jesus said to them, "I am the bread of life;
the one coming to Me never shall hunger."
—John 6:35 BLB

Bread of Life (noun): Something regarded as a source of
spiritual nourishment. —*Online Google Dictionary*

"I am the Bread of Life." Jesus received an incredulous reaction from
the crowd after making this "I Am" pronouncement. As He spoke
to inquisitive followers one Capernaum morning, a hush filled the
room, jaws dropped. The quiet quickly departed as the listeners
shot out indignation and questions.

The night prior to this synagogue declaration, Jesus fed a crowd
of five thousand. Naturally, after witnessing a miracle feeding that
originated with only five loaves of bread and two fish, the crowd
was ultra-curious about this teacher. Some called Him Rabbi. Who
was this wonder from Nazareth telling them He was bread—*the*
source of spiritual nourishment?

Christ's words were perplexing and yes, even scandalous. Even
to His disciples. John 6:60 quotes the disciples, saying, "This is very
hard to understand. How can anyone accept it?"

This is puzzling theology. Is he talking metaphorically? How do
we interpret it?

After reading and researching broadly, I have simplified this
concept of Jesus as the Bread of life down to two points to ponder.

1. Food is vital for life. As is Christ. Jesus claimed that to
    the one who eats this bread accepts His gift of salvation,
    and will live forever (see John 6:51).

2. The previous night, Christ acted out a real-life parable in the feeding of the five thousand. The bread, a symbol for Himself in the life of a believer, delivered physical fullness. Yet, as we know, this stuffed sensation is fleeting, so we must eat again. However, the fullness that Christ gives lasts. It assuages our pain and sin and feeds our emptiness as nothing else can.

Dear Reader, where do you find yourself this Christmastime? Running on empty, or full?

I struggle, swept up in the buying, eating, and decorating. These fun and festive doings are not wrong. However, when I attempt to fill myself with these activities (and I often do), hollowness echoes inside. I mollify pain, emptiness, tiredness, or insecurity. Temporary satisfaction. Downright gluttony.

Only He can satisfy. With Jesus as our holiday priority, gluttony gives way to holy fullness. Oh, how delicious the taste.

Reflection

1. Search your heart. What are you seeking this Advent? The Bread of Life, or something that only gives temporary satisfaction?

2. Read the Eucharist passage, John 6:1–14. Contemplate in prayer.

Prayer

Dear Bread of Life, this Advent time, I choose You and You alone to fill me. I confess my struggles with materialism, greed, and filling myself with things and activities that never satisfy. Nudge me when I slip. Remind me that in You, I will never hunger.
Amen

Break Thou the Bread of Life

Mary A. Lathbury, 1877
[Verses 1 and 4]

Break thou the bread of life,

O Lord, to me,

as thou didst break the loaves

beside the sea.

Beyond the sacred page

I seek thee Lord;

my spirit longs for thee,

O living Word!

Bless thou the bread of life

to me, to me,

as thou didst bless the loaves

by Galilee;

then shall all bondage cease,

all fetters fall;

and I shall find my peace,

my all in all.

December 6
Jesus

And behold, thou shalt conceive in thy womb,
and bring forth a son, and shalt call his name Jesus.
—Luke 1:31 ASV

Iēsoús—Jesus, the transliteration of the Hebrew, which
means "Yahweh saves" (or "Yahweh is salvation").
—*Strong's Exhaustive Concordance*

Yeshua. A common male, Jewish name. A popular name like Jack,
Jake, or John. We discover ten men named Yeshua in the Old Testament. In the New Testament, three other Yeshuas (besides the Savior) hide in the stories. Perhaps in the Bible times, a Yeshua resided
in each neighborhood.

Mary and Joseph, instructed by the angel, gave their uncommon
baby a common name:

"Eight days later, when the baby was circumcised, he was
named Jesus, the name given him by the angel even before he was
conceived" (Luke 2:21 NLT).

The prophets titled Jesus with many names, designations, and
descriptions. Every prophet predicted this Savior. Four hundred
dark and oppressive years spanned between the final words of hope
in the Old Testament and the appearance of the angel (Matthew
1:20) in the early portion of the New Testament. Then, Jesus arrived
on the scene.

An interminable wait.

Blackness and oppression had settled on this nation of Jews. Yet
I believe the hope of their rescuer filled the dark with flickers of
light. Expectation was in the air they breathed, the anticipation of a

not-so-normal rescuer they had been promised.

Then, along came the savior-baby, this long-expected Jesus, given a normal, humble name: Yeshua.

In Philippians 2:7–8 (*Voice*), the Apostle Paul describes Jesus as "a servant in form and a man indeed. The very likeness of humanity, He humbled Himself . . ."

There is a key in this passage as to why God may have chosen this humble name for His noble son. You see, our Jesus lowered Himself from the glory of God and all of its uncommon aspects, to live with us here, in all of its common aspects. A humble human. A king with a heart to live as a regular "Jake" for us in our neighborhood. Nothing flashy or arrogant about this Yeshua, not even his name. One who knew our suffering, pain, poverty, and expectation. A Savior with a non-glamorous name, come to save a non-glamorous world.

How I love the name Jesus, the name above all names! It will never be common to me.

Reflection

1. In what practical ways might you model the humility of Jesus this season?

2. Read Philippians 2:5–12. Journal your thoughts on this passage.

Prayer

Jesus, I praise Your earthly name, so common for an uncommon Savior. I humble myself before You this Advent day as I thank You for humbling yourself so commonly for me. I love You, my Jesus. The name above all names.

Amen

Come, Though Long Expected Jesus

Charles Wesley, 1744
[Verse 1]

Come, thou long expected Jesus,

born to set thy people free;

from our fears and sins release us,

let us find our rest in thee.

Israel's strength and consolation,

hope of all the earth thou art;

dear desire of every nation,

joy of every longing heart.

December 7
Christ the Lord

For unto you is born this day in the city of David
a Savior, who is Christ the Lord.
—Luke 2:11 ESV

Christ: God in the flesh, anointed
Lord: Ruler
—*Merriam-Webster* online

Why did God choose to send the angel to the shepherds that night? They probably wondered as well. These were humble, pastural guardians minding their own business. Average people, marginalized, without political power, money or appeal.

So much like us. People needing a loving ruler to lead and guide. To rescue. To save.

After four hundred years of silence, when God spoke again, He opted to speak to people without status: Zechariah, Mary, Joseph, and the shepherds. This story of Christ the Lord plays out among normal humans to whom we can relate.

The angel stood in front of the transfixed shepherds and proclaimed Christ's arrival. The glory of God shone on them as a spotlight of radiance.

This new Ruler was born for all people, not as a Lord of power and clout, but as a baby birthed naturally to a young woman.

I cannot help but think the shepherds' hearts were prepared, because once they witnessed the heavenly light, and then heard the message, they bravely responded and left immediately to meet the baby Jesus.

I picture them as they scurried along, exclaiming, "Come let us adore Him!"

After they worshiped and adored the infant king, these shepherds left to tell others the magnificent news. The first evangelists.

As the shepherds may have, do you wonder why God has chosen you? Has he selected you to parent a special needs child? Has he called you to stay in a loveless marriage? To befriend a prickly coworker? To lead an organization?

Others needing to know Christ the Lord surround us. People desperate for a Savior, who crave shepherd-evangelists to tell them the story. People hungry to see Jesus-in-the-flesh in *us*.

Now is the time. Christmas lends itself to hearts prepared to hear. God has chosen you for a particular task this Advent. Do you know what it is?

> Christ the Lord: "magnificent appellation!"
> —J. A. Bengel

Reflection

1. Can you say from your heart that Jesus is your Lord, Ruler, and Master?

2. How will you adore Him this Advent season?

Prayer

Dear Christ the Lord, give me the power to show others Christ in the flesh this Christmas season. Place people in my life who need to see Your love displayed. Prepare my heart to adore You. Change me as I focus on You. May You become my Lord, Ruler and Master. I am all in.

Amen

Adeste Fideles (O Come, All Ye Faithful)

John Francis Wade, 1744
[Verse 1]

O come, all ye faithful, joyful and triumphant!

O come ye, O come ye to Bethlehem

Come and behold him

Born the King of Angels:

[Chorus]

O come, let us adore Him

O come, let us adore Him

O come, let us adore Him

Christ the Lord

December 8
Son of God

The beginning of the gospel of Jesus Christ,
the Son of God . . .
—Mark 1:1 KJV

So the holy one to be born will be called the Son of God.
—Luke 1:35

Son of God: To call Christ the Son of God is to assert his
true and proper divinity. The second person of the Trinity,
because of his eternal reaction to the first Person, is the
Son of God . . . this title is a claim of equality with God.
—Kingjamesbibleonline/Son-of-God.php4

Radical. Audacious. Blasphemous. How dare He!

Leviticus 24:6 orders death by stoning to anyone who
blasphemes the name of the Lord. Blasphemy is the act of speaking
irreverently about God, claiming equality with God, or claiming to
be God. In John 10:31 we read that the Jews (Jesus's own people)
took up rocks to stone Jesus for making Himself equal with God, by
calling God His father, and for saying, "I and the Father are One."
This long-expected Savior was *not* what the people expected.

> A thing long expected takes the form of the unexpected
> when at last it comes.—Mark Twain

The Jews of the time were an anguished people group. They
suffered under the heavy hand of Rome, and their own religious
leaders.

They put enormous expectation in a future Savior who would come as a king, political ruler, and conqueror. They believed this new leader would restore their political power to its rightful place. He would lift their oppression, bring peace to their land, and punish those who had tormented them for so long.

How dare this seemingly regular, yet audacious person from the Nazareth hood come and mess with their expectation? How dare He accept the title, "Son of God"?

If I strode upon the dusty streets in the sandals of these Jews, would I have felt confusion, distress, and rage? Would I have called this radical man a blasphemer? Would I have picked up a rock? Possibly.

God begat His son, His exact representation on earth, through Mary. Christ was and is a servant and shepherd of peace, grace, sacrifice, and yes, controversy—but not blasphemy. This Son of God came to restore the wayward Jew, reconcile Roman oppressors, and call all humankind to Himself through the forgiveness of sins.

Radical. Audacious. Son of God.

Reflection

1. Read: Psalm 2:7 and Hebrews 5:5. How would your world look today without God's Son?

2. What are your holiday hopes and expectations? Record your thoughts as a prayer.

Prayer

Dear Son of God, You are the expected unexpected. I thank You for forgiving the sins of all humankind, and even me. I thank You for coming in Your unexpected and controversial way. To You the Son of God, be the honor and glory this Advent time and forever.
Amen

Gentle Mary Laid Her Child Down

Joseph Simpson Cook, 1919
[Verse 3]

Gentle Mary laid her child

Lowly in a manger;

He is still the undefiled,

But no more a stranger.

Son of God of humble birth,

Beautiful the story;

Praise His name in all the earth,

Hail! The King of Glory!

December 9
Son of Man

I continued watching in the night visions, and I saw One
like a son of man coming with the clouds of heaven.
He approached the Ancient of Days
and was escorted before Him.
—Daniel 7:13 HCSB

For it has been determined that the Son of Man must die.
—Jesus, in Luke 22:22, NLT

Son of Man: Jesus called Himself the Son of Man many times.
The name means that Jesus is a real man and that He is the
One God promised to send in Daniel 7:13. —*What the Bible Is All About*

Mary, Did You Know?

Mary's babe, beautifully human in her arms. His cries pierce the air. Ten fingers and ten toes all in place. What did she know? Told by an angel she would birth a king. However, as far as we know, God did not tell Mary what was to come: the beatings, the cross and the resurrection. It seems Mary lived each day trusting God with her tomorrows.

Mary's boy-turned-man called Himself the "Son of Man" seventy-eight times. Never the "Son of God." His usual approach humble and subtle. A relatable king. One tempted yet without sin. Divinity and humanity wrapped in a mother's arms. Mary saw it all. The miracles and major events. Eventually she did know.

Would this young mama nursing her newborn *want* to know what was to come? I don't think so. Would you?

So, how about you and I? What do we know? Thankfully, we cannot see into the future on earth. No foretaste of the fate of our own children or loved ones. No preview of pains and joys on the path ahead. Yet, the Bible does give a glimpse of our eternal future via the Son of Man:

> When the Son of Man comes in His glory,
> and all the angels with Him, He will sit on His glorious throne.
> —Matthew 25:31 BSB

> . . . to bring salvation to those who are waiting for Him.
> —Hebrews 9:28 BSB

Like Mary, on this Advent day what we do know is that we may trust our Savior with our tomorrows. The child that Mary delivered, delivered her, and He delivers us too.

Reflection

1. What future unknown will you begin to trust God with today?

2. With eyes closed, picture the Son of Man. What comfort comes to mind?

Prayer

Son of Man, thank You for coming to earth as a human. A baby. You understand my every mortal weakness and struggle. Thank You for what I know and do not know regarding my future. In addition, for the certainty of eternity that waits for me, filled with You.
Amen

Come Thou Omniscient Son of Man

Charles Wesley, 1700s
[Verses 1 and 5]

Come, thou omniscient Son of man,

Display thy sifting power;

Come, with thy Spirit's winnowing fan,

And thoroughly purge thy floor.

Then let us all thy fullness know,

From every sin set free;

Saved to the utmost, saved below,

And perfected in thee.

December 10
Branch of
Righteousness

In those days, and at that time, will I cause
a Branch of righteousness to grow up unto David;
and he shall execute judgment and righteousness in the land.
—Jeremiah 33:15 ERV

Branch: A division of a main stem, supporting the leaves.
Righteous: Applied to God, the perfection or holiness of his
nature. —*Webster's Dictionary 1828* online

The prophet Jeremiah mentions Jesus eight times. Twice he calls
Him "the Branch of righteousness." An unusual term of endearment
these days. When did you last hear someone described as "a branch
of righteousness"? Ever? Me neither.

The Message version says in Jeremiah 33:14–18:

> Watch for this: The time is coming—God's Decree—"when
> I will keep the promise I made to the families of Israel and
> Judah. When that time comes, I will make *a fresh and true shoot
> sprout from the David-Tree ... He will set things right.* The motto for
> the city will be, 'God Has Set Things Right for Us.' " God has
> made it clear that there will always be a descendant of David
> ruling the people of Israel.

Jesus is the "Fresh and true shoot sprout from the David-
Tree." Still not modern-day vernacular, but easier to understand.
The Old Testament foretells Jesus coming to us through the line

of King David. In Matthew chapter one, the genealogy begins with Abraham and ends with Jesus. It is an amazing line of "Who's Who" and "Who Was That?" of Bible celebrity.

However—and this just gets me—because of Christ, *we too* are now on that prized list, because Christ grafted us to Him. As Christians, and children of Abraham, we continue the family line as we sprout His righteousness.

Let us press on through this Christmas time as a people grafted to The Branch of Righteousness, and a legacy of David's tree, as we cultivate the love and message of God. He is the Righteous Vine, and we are the branches.

Reflection

1. Read Matthew 1:1–17 and add your name to the bottom of the list.

2. In John 15:5, Jesus tells us that He is the vine, and we are the branches. Read this verse aloud to Jesus, thanking Him for this truth.

Prayer

Dear Branch of Righteousness, I thank You today for grafting me into Your family line. You make me righteous. You are the most-worthy Vine. Apart from You, I can do nothing. I will be grateful for Your love for me all of the days of my life.

Amen

How Brightly Shines the Morning Star

Philipp Nicolai, 1597
German Christmas Hymn
[Verse 1]

How greatly shines the Morning Star,

With mercy beaming from afar;

The host of heav'n rejoices;

O Righteous Branch, O Jesse's Rod!

Thou Son of Man and Son of God!

We too will lift our voices;

Jesus, Jesus!

Holy, Holy!

Yet most lowly,

Draw Thou near us;

Great Emmanuel, come hear us.

December 11
Lamb of God

The next day John saw Jesus coming toward him and said,
"Look, the Lamb of God, who takes away the sin of the world!"
—John 1:29

Lamb of God: A Christian term for Jesus, first used in the
Gospel of John. It carries out the image of the Crucifixion and
Resurrection of Jesus as a new Passover: a lamb was killed for
the Jewish Passover, and Jesus Himself, in the sacrifice of His
death and Resurrection, is the Lamb for the new Passover.
—*Dictionary.com*

A lamb. The idea seems crazy to us today: animal sacrifice in exchange for our wrong doings, our sins. Yet, from the earliest of Jewish culture, the sacrifice of lambs played a significant part in everyday life, including Passover (See Exodus, 12) and daily temple
sacrifice (see Exodus 29:38–41).

The ancient prophets Isaiah and Jeremiah predicted Jesus as the
ultimate Lamb of God and called Him so: "I was like a lamb being
led to the slaughter" (Jeremiah 11:19 NLT). "He was oppressed, and
He was afflicted, Yet He did not open His mouth; Like a lamb that
is led to slaughter, And like a sheep that is silent before its shearers,
so He did not open His mouth" (Isaiah 53:7 NASB).

It is hard to get our heads around it—the God of the Universe
placed His Son, this perfect Lamb, on an altar (the cross) to die. The
ultimate ransom for *our* wrong doings. The perfect One in place of
imperfect us.

Now, what about us? Do you feel damaged, incapacitated by sin this Christmas time? We, the poor in spirit. The lonely and the lost. The addict. What does Christ's sacrifice mean for us? Where does our future land?

In 1 Peter 1:18–21, *The Message* says:

> Your life is a journey you must travel with a deep con-sciousness of God . . . He paid with Christ's sacred blood . . . He died like an unblemished, sacrificial lamb. And this was no afterthought . . . God always knew he was going to do this for you. It's because of this sacrificed Messiah, whom God then raised from the dead and glorified, that you trust God, that you know you have a future in God.

Hallelujah! Because of this perfect Lamb, we have a future in God. Because of Him, we seek healing.

May we, the broken, sacrifice our pride, our hurt, our . . . (fill in the blank) as a Christmas gift to God and others, by taking a first step to mend whatever needs reconciliation in our lives.

Reflection

1. Our sin separates us from God. What does this mean?
    See Romans 6:23

2. With hands upturned, offer yourself to God, thank Him for the sacrifice of His Lamb.

Prayer

Lamb of God, thank You for being the ultimate and perfect sacrifice. This Christmas, my gift to You is me.
Amen

The Lamb of God

Author: T. S. M.,
translated by Frances Bevan, 1899
[Verse 1]

Lamb, Thy white-robed people feeding

’Neath the shadowing wings—

Lamb, Thy weary, thirsty leading,

To the living springs.

Once upon the altar bleeding,

Now on God’s high throne—

Unto Thee salvation, glory,

Lamb of God, alone.

December 12
Image of the
Invisible God

Jesus answered, ". . . Anyone who has seen Me
has seen the Father."
—John 14:9

The Son is the image of the invisible God,
the firstborn over all creation.
—Colossians 1:15

Christ in his human nature is the visible discovery of the
invisible God, and he that hath seen Him hath seen the Father.
—Matthew Henry Commentary (from Colossians 1:15–23)

Early in John 14, we read of an exchange between Jesus and two of
his disciples. I picture the group as they walk along a dusty road;
the sizzling sun shining on their faces as they speak earnestly to
one another.

In verse eight, Phillip asks Jesus to show them the Father. Jesus
responds to Phillip, "Anyone who has seen me, has seen the Father"
(v. 9).

Say what? No, that is not what Phillip said, but I would have.
I may have asked Jesus for more clarification. Something like, "You
mean, when I look at your face, I see God? The creator of the world?
The author of life and death?"

Heaven presented the disciples with a beautiful gift: The Father
revealed Himself in human form, radiating His glory through His

son. These earthly followers saw, touched, cried with, and lived with God in the flesh.

So many moments in my life, I have wished for Jesus's presence in human form: His hand to hold, His arms to embrace while he dries my tears, and His smile to nudge me along when I am unsure.

Paul tells us further in Colossians 1:15, "The Son is the image of the invisible God . . ." The Greek word used for image here is *Eikon*. "The word involves the two ideas of representation and manifestation" (*Vines Expository Dictionary of New Testament Words* [Reformed Church Publications: Zeeland, MI], p. 520).

God represented and manifested Himself through our Savior. It started with the babe growing in Mary's womb, to the infant in the manger, to the man walking with his friends. Then, finally the rescuer on the cross and resurrected King. This boggles my brain, but infuses my heart with joy.

Join me in looking to this manifested representation of God at Christmas. God's gift to us. An incomprehensible, miraculous gift.

Reflection

1. What is the image of God in your mind? Write it down using vivid words.

2. Read and meditate on Hebrews 1:3 and 1 Timothy 1:17.

Prayer

Dear Image of the Invisible God, unlike the disciples, I do not have You in human form, walking with me. I look with joyful anticipation to the moment I behold Your face and touch Your hands. Your word gives me numerous descriptions, allowing me to paint a picture of You in my mind. This holiday time, I thank You for the gift of your Son, who represented and manifested Your glory. Your image.

Amen

Immortal, Invisible, God Only Wise

Walter Chambers Smith, 1867
[Verses 1 and 3]

Immortal, invisible, God only wise,

In light inaccessible hid from our eyes,

Most blessed, most glorious, the Ancient of Days,

Almighty, victorious, thy great name we praise.

Great Father of glory, pure Father of Light,

Thine angels adore thee, all veiling their sight;

All praise we would render; O help us to see

'Tis only the splendor of light hideth thee!

December 13
King of Kings and Lord of Lords

And on His robe and on His thigh He has a name written,
"King of Kings and Lord of Lords."
—Revelation 19:16 NASB

King of Kings and Lord of Lords: Denoting the sovereign power and authority which He had. This He always had, but He now comes forth openly to manifest it.—*Matthew Pool Commentary*

Herod the Great. Herod the Tyrant. The king of Palestine at the time of Jesus's birth was a hateful, vengeful, jealous and greedy king. A slaughterer of baby boys.

> Herod had two important attributes: absolute loyalty to Rome, and political prowess, which he exercised with extraordinary brutality by extirpating all signs of opposition, even within his own family . . . This earned him the saying attributed to Augustus: "It is better to be Herod's pig than his son."
> —Myjewishlearning.com

This was *not* the king the Jews had been promised. An oppressed people, living under the heel of the Roman Empire. They hoped, waited, and pined for their true king. A true king is righteous, deserving the highest authority, sovereign and royal. A true Lord is a master, one who reigns supreme. Herod plotted to destroy Mary's baby, the true King (see Matthew 2:16–18), and was not the last to do so.

In Revelation 19, we read that heaven will open, and Christ the King will ride out of the clouds on a white horse. This royal Ruler will have letters written on His robe and thigh. Inscribed on both, the words "King of Kings and Lord of Lords."

The church waits in expectation. As in the time of Herod, wickedness roams the earth today. Sometimes oppression and blackness creep into the cracks and crevices of family life, our emotions, and our holidays. As we look toward Christ's return, may we expose the shadowed places that grip us. As a church, we need to reach out in hope and community, and share the light of our King to every burdened soul.

One day, Christ alone will reign supreme as King of Kings and Lord of Lords. His royal splendor will uncover every dark shadow and ring in freedom.

Let loving hearts enthrone Him.

Reflection

1. Read Revelation 19:6–10. Read it again, this time aloud as a praise to the true King.

2. Are you living "under the heel" of oppression or pain? I pray this Christmas will be a season of freedom as you allow God to reign as your King of Kings and Lord of Lords!

Prayer

King of Kings and Lord of Lords, You are the healer of my oppression and pain. Until the time of your physical return, I allow You to reign in my heart. My one true King and Lord.

Amen

What Child Is This?

William C. Dix, 1865
[Verse 3]

So bring Him incense, gold, and myrrh,

Come, peasant, king to own Him.

The King of Kings salvation brings;

Let loving hearts enthrone Him.

[Chorus]

This, this is Christ the King

Whom shepherds guard and angels sing.

Haste, haste to bring Him laud,

The Babe, the Son of Mary.

December 14
Word Made Flesh

And the Word was made flesh, and dwelt among us,
(and we beheld his glory, the glory as of the
only begotten of the Father) full of grace and truth.
—John 1:14 KJV

Calling Jesus "the Word" implies that He is
"God-Expressing-Himself." To us.
—John Piper, The *Dawning of Indestructible Joy*

Everything changed when the Word lived among us. The idea that God's Word became flesh through Jesus strains my brain. A complicated concept to unpack. I adore the beautiful imagery given by John Piper: God expressing Himself to us.

To explore this concept, let's examine the Word Made Flesh in two parts: Jesus as the *Word* of the Old Testament, and Jesus as the *Flesh* of the New Testament.

In the beginning was the Word (John 1:1). This Word, this Son of God, existed before His time on earth. Christ was before *all* things, the second person of the Trinity. Christ was present at creation, He was part of creation, and He is the Creator (see Colossians 1:16 and Hebrews 1:2).

Christ is the Jehovah of the ancient Scriptures, the eternal Word. Before His time on earth, Hebrew prophets foretold the coming Messiah (the Word who would become Flesh). Hundreds of Messianic prophecies were fulfilled through Christ. Here are just a few of them:

The Messiah would:

- Be born of a virgin (Micah 5:2; Matthew 2:1)
- Live in Egypt for a time (Hosea 11:1; Matthew 2:14–15)
- Experience horrific rejection by the Jews (Isaiah 53:3; John 1:11)
- Be resurrected from the dead (Psalm 49:15; Acts 2:22–32)

God expressed Himself to us through the words of prophecy. Then, came the Messiah! God's in-the-flesh-love-letter to us. Christ, the fulfillment of the Old Testament promises, wrapped in swaddling clothes. Those ancient words, made flesh and blood.

Christ *dwelt* here. As the Greek translates, He *tabernacled* with us. This symbolic word evokes the imagery of a central place of worship, or human fellowship with God. For thirty-three years Jesus of Nazareth walked on this earth and fulfilled the law of the Old Testament. Every single prophecy realized. This baby, this Word Made Flesh, changed everything.

Reflection

1. What does "The Word Made Flesh" mean to you? How will the Word who became flesh enlighten your Christmas season?

2. Read the prophetic Scripture listed above under "The Messiah would . . ." Record your observations.

Prayer

Dear Word Made Flesh, You changed everything! You are God's word, manifest in flesh. You dwelt among the likes of us, like us, yet sinless. Thank You for fulfilling hundreds of prophecies and for expressing Yourself to me this Christmas through your letter of love, born in the manger.

Amen

The Word Made Flesh

Unknown
[Verses 1 and 2]

The Word made Flesh, right reverently,

The rising of our Sun, we sing,

Of Mary born with us to be

Emmanuel, our God and King.

Good news! The book of Life's unsealed,

To men on earth His peace He brings,

Through ages promised, now revealed,

He comes with healing on His wings.

December 15
Banner of Salvation

In that day the heir to David's throne will be a
Banner of Salvation to all the world.
—Isaiah 11:10 NLT

Banner (noun): A square flag; a military ensign; the principal
standard of a prince or state. —*Webster's 1828 Dictionary online*

Jehovah Nissi: Jehovah (God) is my Banner.
—Biblestudytools.org

His Banner over Me Is Love

Grace Camp, my childhood church camp in the Arizona
Mountains, is where I first gave my heart to Jesus. Warm memories
fill me of those days: boats on the lake, hikes, flashlight wars, metal
bunks, giggling at midnight, underdone pancakes, skits, and songs.

"His Banner Over Me Is Love"

As we sang this song at Grace Camp, my child's mind imagined
the love of Jesus as a football-field-sized flag, waving protectively
over me. As a woman, I reflect on how true my childhood image of
Jesus has proven itself in my life. Little did my girl-self know that
these lyrics would play in my head in the darkest moments of my
life's journeys, reminding me that Jesus is still here, covering me
with love and protection.

Isaiah tells us in chapter 11 that God will gather His people from
the four corners of the earth. In verse 10 we learn that Jesus will be a
Banner to the entire world. In verse twelve the idea continues: "He

will raise a flag among the nations and assemble the exiles of Israel. He will gather the scattered people of Judah from the ends of the earth" (NLT).

Our Messiah, the Banner, is deep rooted where all peoples of the world may come to find love, restoration, and eternal salvation. Not just me, not just you, but also the entire world. The invitation is for all. My mind reels at the notion.

This concept is especially remarkable as we push through the Christmas Crazies. The heir to David's throne adores you. He is your banner of love and salvation. Picture Him as your deep-rooted flag this Christmas, flying proudly over you, whispering words of love.

In turn, let us bear His flag. March your Jesus-flag through the holidays. Bring his love and message of salvation to the four corners of your world.

Reflection

1. To whom in your corner of the world will you share the truth of salvation?

2. Read these Scriptures aloud as a praise: Habakkuk 2:14; Psalm 22:27; Psalm 86:9 and Revelation 3:7.

Prayer

Dear Banner of Salvation, fill my mind with pictures of Your salvation-banner waving beautifully at Christmas time and each day of the year. Thank You for loving this big old world and for the hope of Salvation. I love You, Jesus.

Amen

His Banner over Me Is Love

Unknown
[Verse 1]

The Lord is mine and I am His,

His banner over me is love.

The Lord is mine and I am His,

His banner over me is love.

The Lord is mine and I am His,

His banner over me is love.

His banner over me is love.

December 16
Man of Sorrows

He was despised and rejected—a man of sorrows,
acquainted with deepest grief.
We turned our backs on him and looked the other way.
He was despised, and we did not care.
—Isaiah 53:3 NLT

Man of Sorrows (noun): In Christian exegesis,
an appellation of Jesus Christ as the suffering Savior.
—*Dictionary.com*

Christmastime. A beautiful, festive season: Carols play in the shops, lights twinkle on trees, big bows tied on boxes with glossy paper, cookies and candies, and *all* of the food! Precious little girls with their hair curled, in velvet dresses and shiny shoes. Much of the Western world is clothed in its finest to celebrate.

However, in searching for meaning in the season, for the reason for this season, peel away the glamour and frivolity and find a baby in a manger. Nothing beautiful, nothing festive surrounded Him. A tiny babe with no clothes in a sorrowful place: dirty, foul-smelling animals, a dark cave, no female attendants for Mary, and no uncles gathered with Joseph to smoke congratulatory cigars. Perhaps a foreshadowing of what was to come for this child: A life of sorrows that began in the cradle and ended on the cross.

Consider the following:

1. After His birth, King Herod hunted Him, seeking to murder Him. (Matthew 2:1–8)
2. Jesus's parents fled to Egypt to hide. (Matthew 2:13–23)
3. Jesus suffered temptation by Satan. (Luke 4:2–13, Hebrews 2:18)

4. During His ministry, Jesus endured persecution from the religious leaders. (Mark 3:6; Mark 11:27–12:17)
5. Also, willfulness (Luke 9:46), denial (John 18:13–27), and betrayal from His disciples. (Mark 14:10–11)
6. His sweat turned to blood as He wept in the Garden of Gethsemane. (Luke 22:44)
7. He was beaten, flogged, mocked, and hung on a cross. Broken by grief. (Matthew 27:1–54)

Our suffering Savior did all this for love. Because of love, the infant became a Man of Sorrows and embraced our suffering in His earthly life, so that we may embrace His eternal splendor. A holy exchange. May we live as people of joy, clothed in His finest, as we celebrate the real meaning of Christmas.

Hallelujah what a Savior!

Reflection

1. Set aside time to look up today's Scriptures, and consider Christ's immense love in suffering for you.

2. What sorrows are you experiencing this season? Kneel before your Savior and release them.

Prayer

Dear Man of Sorrows, I kneel before the manger; how beautiful and sorrowful it is. I lay down my sorrows of the season before You, as I remember You were born to bear them. Thank You for choosing an earthly life of sorrow, so that I may be a person of joy, clothed in Your finest!

Amen

"Man of Sorrows" What a Name

Author: P. P. Bliss, 1875
[Verses 1 and 3]

Man of sorrows, what a name

For the Son of God, who came

Ruined sinners to reclaim:

Hallelujah, what a Savior!

Guilty, helpless, lost were we;

Blameless Lamb of God was he,

Sacrificed to set us free:

Hallelujah, what a Savior!

December 17
Prince of Peace

For to us a child is born, to us a son is given,
and the government will be on his shoulders.
And he will be called Wonderful Counselor,
Mighty God, Everlasting Father, Prince of Peace.
—Isaiah 9:6

Shalom: A Hebrew word meaning peace, harmony,
wholeness, completeness, prosperity, welfare and tranquility.
—*Online Google Dictionary*

Of all the names of Jesus, Prince of Peace is my favorite. When I consider the word prince, my mind conjures up handsomeness, dignity, and nobility. A son of a king, who plays the gentler, more peaceful role of ruling. My little-girl vision of Cinderella's prince is whom I see.

Our Prince of Peace is full of gentleness and nobility as well. And this Ruler grants shalom *in* and *through* us.

As a Christ follower, I have access to wholeness and peace. The Prince of Peace lives inside me. Yet, I often lack tranquility. As a mom of four sons, I worry about them. I get busy and hurried as life presses in. Anxiety over money and grown-up life can overtake me. That is when I *stop* and stay my soul on Jesus. When I get still, His clarity and shalom wash over me. I access this Shalom as I center myself in Him, breathe in His peace, and read His words.

Because of this gift from my Prince, I in turn offer His Shalom to the world around me. It is not always apparent, but God *is* ushering in His kingdom here on earth, through His Church. Part of His call on our lives is to marshal His shalom into a chaotic and hurting world. Little pieces of peace on earth.

Christmas time provides countless opportunities to pilot peace. People are often gentler and open to the Savior's message this time of year, more receptive to love and Shalom. Additionally, this season can be a period of tremendous grief and utter pain. Hurting hearts and needs abound. For such a time as this, we are here on assignment for our Prince.

Join me as we worship Him inwardly this Advent as Prince of Peace. And outwardly present Him to a hurting world.

Reflection

1. Take time to stay your soul today. Breathe deeply as Shalom washes over you.

2. Write a list of the ways you might pilot peace in the chaos around you.

Prayer

Prince of Peace, I invite Your Shalom to wash over me today. As I breathe it in, I thank You that I am whole in You. I will be an instrument of Your peace to the world around me this Christmas.
Amen

Hark! The Herald Angels Sing

Charles Wesley, 1739
[Verse 3]

Hail the heaven-born Prince of Peace!

Hail the Sun of Righteousness!

Light and life to all He brings,

Risen with healing in His wings;

Mild, He lays his glory by,

Born that man no more may die,

Born to raise the sons of earth,

Born to give them second birth:

[Refrain]

Hark! The herald angels sing

Glory to the newborn King.

December 18
The Resurrection
and the Life

Jesus said to her, "I am the resurrection and the life.
Whoever believes in me, though he die, yet shall he live."
—John 11:25 ESV

Resurrection (noun): The act of rising from the dead.

Life (noun): The animate existence or period of animate
existence of an individual.—*Dictionary.com*

A resurrection story. You may know it, but if you do not, I encourage you to read John 11:1–44. As we drop into a conversation between Jesus and Martha, we hear the Savior say in verse 25, "I Am the Resurrection and the Life." Then in verse 26, Jesus asks Martha, "Do you believe this?"

This is a bold declaration and a crucial question. A question we must ask ourselves: "Do I believe?"

The book of John contains seven "I Am" statements. Through these astonishing proclamations, Jesus attests to His God-nature. Christ makes the claim that He is the hope and new life for the Jews. When Jesus says, "*I Am* the Resurrection and the Life," He draws a line between Himself and the God of the Old Testament. The God who said to Moses, "*I AM WHO I AM*" (Exodus 3:14).

Because of His death and resurrection, we, too, are reborn to abundant life on earth and in eternity, once we choose to follow this Savior. As a miraculous result, the power that lives in Jesus lives in us. When Christ died, we died, and when He rose from the dead, we, too, rose (see Romans 3:6–7).

> Jesus is life and power. Jesus gives life and power. Remember that He who rose from the dead, rose to pour out His Holy Spirit into human lives, and, by that Spirit, to make available to any individual all the fullness of Himself, twenty-four hours a day. —Ray C. Stedman

Return with me now to the question Jesus asks, "Do you believe this?" May we answer as Martha: "Yes, Lord, I believe that you are the Christ, the Son of God who was to come into the world" (John 11:27 ESV).

Dear reader, do you believe this?

Reflection

1. For further study: Exodus 23:21; Isaiah 44:6; Ephesians 2:1–10; Colossians 3:1–4; and 1 Thessalonians 4:13, 14.

2. How might your day, your life, and your Christmas change if you truly believed that His resurrection power lives in you?

Prayer

Dear Resurrection and the Life, I declare to you this Advent day that I believe You are the Christ. Come to give me abundant life! I live under grace and freedom, and I believe that Your power lives in me, twenty-four hours a day. This Christmas I celebrate these truths. Today, I put on my clothes of new life, and I walk in shoes of resurrected hope and faith.

Amen

Morning Light

Shaker music, 1893
author unknown
[Verse 1]

The resurrection angels call,

Awaken is the cry!

The earth is filled with morning light;

The clouds of darkness fly!

This is the day of righteousness,

For now has Christ appeared!

Behold, upon the mountain height,

His snowy banner reared!

December 19
Lord of the Sabbath

For the Son of Man is Lord of the Sabbath.
—Matthew 12:8

Sabbath (as a verb) is first mentioned in the Genesis creation narrative, where the seventh day is set aside as a day of rest (in Hebrew, *shabbath*), and made holy by God (Genesis 2:2, 3).—*Wikipedia.org*

Sabbath (noun): time of rest.
—*Webster's 1828 Dictionary* online

As the mom of four, wife of one, and the main orchestrator of the Saatzer Christmas, I admit the holidays were a draining undertaking for many years, and I am to blame. You see, I was an eager mom when my littles were little. I was enthusiastic as I started our traditions as a family. Oh. So. Enthusiastic. I started book-reading traditions, cooking traditions, cookie-baking traditions, gift-deliveries-to-neighbors traditions, taking the boys on dates traditions, and so much more. I bet you feel tired reading this. Me too.

In the beginning, little did I know how much the boys would adore these events. Little did I know how much these activities would exhaust me. If I missed even one of them, I would hear about it as my kiddos laid on the guilt.

Many nights I would collapse on my bed without having spent one quiet moment in reflection or savoring my Savior during His season.

I needed permission from somewhere or someone to *stop*. Clearly, I was not getting it from my kids. Therefore, I found my permission in God's word. There are three points in particular that communicate just how Jesus is our rest.

1. He beckons us to come to Him for rest. (Matthew 11:28)
2. We see His example in making rest a priority. (Matthew 6:31)
3. He calls Himself the Lord of the Sabbath. (Matthew 12:8)

Sometimes I put a "cease and desist" sign over myself in order for sanity to prevail. Although I do not regret one second spent with my precious sons, looking back, I recognize that I did not need to run myself down to make Christmas successful. Today, I am grateful for the traditions that have woven themselves through the fabric of our family. Yet, once I learned to cease striving, to include solitude and rest, I savored my Christmas and my family in deeper ways. Jesus is our place of quiet rest.

Reflection

1. Are there areas in your life where you want (or need!) to cease striving?

2. Is Jesus your Lord of Sabbath rest?

Prayer

Dear Lord of the Sabbath, I invite You to become my Lord of the Sabbath rest. Not only one day per week, but anytime. Teach me how to rest deeply in you this holiday time, and always.
Amen

There Is a Place of Quiet Rest

Cleland Boyd McAfee, 1903
[Verse 1]

There is a place of quiet rest,

Near to the heart of God,

A place where sin cannot molest,

Near to the heart of God.

[Refrain]

O Jesus, blest Redeemer,

Sent from the heart of God,

Hold us, who wait before Thee,

Near to the heart of God.

December 20
Light of the World

The people walking in darkness have seen a great light; on those living in the land of deep darkness a light has dawned.
—Isaiah 9:2

Again Jesus spoke to them, saying, "I am the light of the world. Whoever follows me will not walk in darkness, but will have the light of life." —John 8:12 ESV

Egō Eimi to Phōs tou Kosmou: "I am the Light of the World."

An astounding claim.

In the temple, Jesus directed these words to chief religious leaders and His own followers. I picture mouths agape as they listened to a mere carpenter, this typical-looking guy from unexciting Nazareth, utter these words. Their minds must have reeled thinking: *Whom does he think he is, calling himself this name? We are in charge here, not him! Such audacity to come in here and act this way!*

This audacious claim made by an audacious Savior.

Fast forward to today, to you and me. How do we get our minds around this astounding claim?

I thought it might benefit us to unpack and ponder this bold Christ-statement. I sliced it into three pieces:

1. Christ is the universal Savior. His light offering is for the entire world. "I am the light of the world" (Jo'

2. Christ is the only Light, the only way to the Fathe 14:6 says: "Jesus answered, 'I am the way and the tru the life. No one comes to the Father except through i

3. Christ's Light shines through us as His light bearers. "Let your light shine before men, that they may see your good deeds and glorify your Father in heaven" (Matthew 5:16 NASB).

So, who *does* He think He is? I, too, stand with my mouth agape like the temple leaders. My mind reels as I contemplate our Savior—the light of Christmas and the answer to every question. This moment, join me in reveling in the glow of Jesus. Take a deep breath and close your eyes. Set a timer for five minutes and experience darkness. Then, as you open your eyes, thank the One who rescued you from blackness to give you an eternity of magnificent light.

Reflection

1. Are there dark places in your heart not yet surrendered to His light?

2. How can you be a light bearer to a dark world this Christmas and beyond?

Prayer

Dear Light of the World, I thank You for shining your light on this dark world, to the very ends of the earth, and into my own heart. I choose to reflect the Light of Your love to my world this season. Speak to me, God; show me how and where I can be a light bearer.

Amen

Jesus the Light of the World

George D. Elderkin, 1890
[Refrain]

We'll walk in the light, beautiful light.

Come where the dewdrops of mercy shine bright.

O, shine all around us by day and by night.

Jesus, the light of the world.

December 21
King of Glory

Who is He, this King of Glory?
The Lord of Hosts—He is the King of Glory. Selah
—Psalm 24:10 BSB

Glory: *Chabod* (Hebrew): Weightiness; honor, splendor, power, wealth, authority, and magnificence

Doxa (Greek): Splendor, radiance, and majesty centered in Jesus —*Strong's Exhaustive Concordance*

Who Is This King of Glory? King David asks this question in Psalm 24, a prophetic and poetic piece of Scripture.

Thousands of years later, I ask the same question.

Who is this King of Glory? *Glory.* Hmmm . . . The glory of God is an abstract concept I somewhat understand, yet struggle to convey. Glory is an attribute of God that I sense and feel, like a painting of magnificent color and light in my imagination. Or, in my mind's eye, I see a majestic golden throne of God, surrounded by angelic beings, their wings of the purest white. A mood of indescribable harmony and completeness fills me.

In my search of Scripture, I found enlightening passages on the topic, as well as insight to our question.

- In Hebrews 1:3 we learn that the Savior is the radiance of God's glory and is God's exact representation.
- John tells us in John 1:14 that the world saw Christ's glory when He walked the earth.
- In 2 Peter 1:17 we read that the Son received glory from His Father.

- Jesus told Mary (in John 11:40) that if she believed, she would see the glory of God.
- Mark writes in Mark 13:26 that we will someday witness the King of Glory coming in clouds of glory and power.

There are further passages to search on this topic, and I encourage you to do so. However, I believe the knowledge and understanding of glory is a concept we will not wholly grasp until heaven, where we will have front row seats to His splendor.

Reflection

1. Who is this King of Glory to you? Journal your thoughts.

2. Open your Bible to Psalm 24 and read it aloud. Picture Jesus seated next to His Father as the Son radiates the Father's Glory.

Prayer

Dear King of Glory, I believe! In this moment, and throughout this day, I fix my eyes on Your glory. Your glory bears weight and authority. You are the splendid, radiant, majestic, and magnificent reflection of the Father. Eternity is too short to adore you, Jesus. We will spend forever worshipping You and never come to the end of Your attributes. I humbly submit and commit myself to giving You glory this Christmas.

Amen

King of Glory, King of Peace

George Herbert, 1633
[Verses 1 and 2]

King of glory, King of peace,

I will love Thee;

And that love may never cease,

I will move Thee.

Thou hast granted my request,

Thou hast heard me;

Thou didst note my working breast,

Thou hast spared me.

Sev'n whole days, not one in sev'n,

I will praise Thee;

in my heart, though not in heav'n,

I can raise Thee.

Small it is, in this poor sort

to enroll Thee:

e'en eternity's too short

to extol Thee.

December 22
Good Shepherd

I am the good shepherd.
The good shepherd lays down his life for the sheep.
—John 10:11

The Good Shepherd is an image used in the periscope of
John 10:1–21, in which Jesus Christ is depicted as the
Good Shepherd who lays down his life for the (His) sheep. —*Wikipedia.org*

Images of sheep and shepherds dot the Bible. In fact, the man after God's own heart, King David, was himself a shepherd. I have yet to see a shepherd in person (besides little people in Christmas programs), but I know they still exist—just not in my neighborhood.

Before I wrote this, I watched online videos of shepherds and their sheep. As the Bible says, we humans truly are like sheep. I saw these cute creatures follow the crowd, scatter in fear, and go astray. The shepherd would seek them out and lead them back to a safe, good pasture under the protection of his gentle care.

Enter the Good Shepherd in John 10. Here, Jesus speaks to a crowd who understood the difference between a good and bad shepherd. Sheep and shepherds were a familiar element of everyday life. So were the religious leaders who were also in the throng. Here, Christ called Himself the Good Shepherd, this term, a powerful yet tender "I am" statement. He contrasts Himself to the religious leaders who were not always tender and good to their followers. This Shepherd of human sheep was unlike any religious leader of the day. His motivation, steeped in love, was a desire to tend to the souls of His fold.

Ultimately, our Shepherd laid His very life down for His lambs.

He gave up His life for His flock, for humankind.

As His precious sheep, we accept that we belong in His fold as we celebrate Christmas. Because He is our guide, we find green pastures in His love this season. We trust Him because His Shepherd gift was the ultimate sacrifice for us, His sheep.

Reflection

1. Read aloud King David's words in Psalm 23; commit this beautiful text to memory if you have not already.

2. Do you follow the Good Shepherd? Have you surrendered yourself to His tender care? If not, do so this day.

Prayer

Dear Good Shepherd, I confess I am sometimes lost, scared, and go astray. Today, I choose You, my shepherd, and follow in Your tender steps. As David did, I proclaim, "The Lord is my shepherd"! I am eternally grateful that You laid Your life down for me. Your love for Your sheep is beyond understanding.

Amen

The King of Love My Shepherd Is

H. W. Baker, 1868
[Verses 1 and 6]

The King of love my shepherd is,

whose goodness faileth never.

I nothing lack if I am his,

and he is mine forever.

And so through all the length of days,

thy goodness faileth never;

Good Shepherd, may I sing thy praise

within thy house forever.

December 23
Emanuel

Behold, a virgin shall be with child, and shall bring forth a
son, and they shall call his name Emmanuel,
which being interpreted is, God with us.
—Matthew 1:23 KJV

Emanuel, **Emmanuel**, or **Immanuel** is a given name
or surname derived from the Hebrew name עמנואל
(*Immanuel*, meaning "God is with us"). —*Wikipedia.org*

On a particularly naughty day, my mom, fed up with my little-girl
antics said, "You can't see Him, but Jesus is here with us. How do
you think He feels when you act like this?" Way to throw down the
Jesus-guilt, mom. Yet her statement resonated with me, causing me
to ponder: *How can Jesus be in heaven and invisibly next to me at the same
time?*

God with us. Emanuel dwelled on earth as a baby, a child, and
then a man. Fully human, but without sin. A baby crying for His
mother. A boy playing with friends in the village of Nazareth. A
man led to a cross to die.

God with us. A miracle-man ministered to by angels, able to
read a person's heart and thoughts. A Healer of souls and flesh. The
Savior of the world.

My mom was correct; Jesus is here, even though we cannot see
Him. With His parting words, Jesus told the church He is with us
always (see Mathew 3:20). The Bible says in 1 Corinthians 3:16 that
God's Spirit lives in us.

Emanuel. Jesus is with us in our battles, in our grief. He is with us in a crowded place, in moments of desperate loneliness. Emanuel joins us in the wilderness, in the valley, in our deepest pain and utmost joy.

My friend, He is here when laughter erupts and when the holidays hurt, when you feel stretched beyond your abilities, as you recline with a good book, or when the pain of loneliness tears at your heart, or as loved ones encircle you. *He is here.* Emanuel. God with us.

Reflection

1. God is with you. Do you believe this as truth?

2. Where do you need Him the most this day? Include Him as you set your priorities, order your finances, or love your naughty kid. Ask Him to meet you here.

Prayer

Emanuel, we claim this truth today: You are God with us. We hold tight to You in our deepest hurts and highest joys. You hold us in our wilderness and pain. You are with us this Christmas and always. Thank You.

Amen

Immanuel

Words by C. H. Spurgeon, 1853
[Verses 1 and 2]

When once I mourned a load of sin;

When conscience felt a wound within;

When all my works were thrown away;

When on my knees I knelt to pray,

Then, blissful hour, remembered well,

I learned Thy love, Immanuel.

When storms of sorrow toss my soul;

When waves of care around me roll;

When comforts sink, when joys shall flee;

When hopeless griefs shall gape for me,

One word the tempest's rage shall quell—

That word, Thy name, Immanuel.

December 24
Messiah

The Spirit of the Sovereign Lord is upon me, for the Lord has
anointed me to bring good news to the poor. He has sent me
to comfort the brokenhearted and to proclaim that captives
will be released and prisoners will be freed.
—Isaiah 61:1 NLT

Messiah: The term "messiah" is the translation of the Hebrew term
Masiah, meaning to smear or anoint. Persons who were anointed
had been elected, designated, appointed, given authority, qualified,
and equipped for specific offices and tasks related to these.
—biblestudytools.com

"Can I hold Messiah?" Our toddler friend Megan called our baby
Josiah "Messiah" when he was brand new. Megan's cute name confusion resounded with me because my Josiah was a December baby.
I cherished those Christmas days, newborn in my arms. Often my
thoughts would wander to the baby Messiah in His mother's arms.
What was it like to hold the real Messiah? To Mary, or anyone else
who admired Him, He looked like a regular baby, just as mine did.
He may have had his mama's eyes, or His grandpa's curly hair. He
cried and needed to eat—a lot. A seemingly normal human.

Yet we know He was not. He was unlike any baby ever born.
This child was God's anointed, the Messiah, worshiped at His birth
by shepherds and angels.

Anointed is a word we do not hear often. The Urban Dictionary
defines anointed this way:

Blessed and called to be great, made with a purpose, honest and pure, set aside for a unique reason. Unshakeable and strong. Predestined to be awesome.

Jesus, the promised Messiah, certainly was predestined to be awesome!

The Promised Messiah was

- proclaimed by John as the promised Messiah at Jesus's baptism (see John 1:29; John 1:32, 34);
- anointed and set above everyone else (see Hebrews 1:9);
- filled with the Holy Spirit (see Acts 10:38).

The baby in a manger, so much like mine. However, He was God and human all in one, the promised and anointed One. This Messiah baby, born for us to worship. Born for us to live for Him and to live because of Him.

Reflection

1. As you go about this Christmas Eve day, breathe silent, worshipful prayers to your Messiah.

2. Purpose to walk tall in your anointing, prepared to share the love of the Messiah.

Prayer

Dear Messiah, on this Christmas Eve, I picture You, the Anointed One, in the arms of Your mother. And I thank You for Your anointing in my life. You made me with a purpose and for a purpose; I, too, am predestined to be awesome. All because of You.

Amen

Angels from the Realms of Glory

James Montgomery, 1816
[Verses 1 and 2]

Angels, from the realms of glory,

Wing your flight o'er all the earth;

Ye who sang creation's story,

Now proclaim Messiah's birth:

Shepherds, in the field abiding,

watching o'er your flocks by night,

God with us is now residing;

yonder shines the infant light

[Chorus]

Come and worship, come and worship

Worship Christ, the newborn King.

December 25
Savior

Sōtếrion (Greek): 1. Saving, bringing salvation;
2. The hope of (future) salvation;
3. He who embodies this salvation, or through whom God is
about to achieve it —Biblestudytools.com

'Tis the Season for the Savior. Today is our last day to savor the Savior
together and I will miss you, my friend. Let's spend our final moments of our Advent journey focused on God's gift. The sole purpose of this gift was deliverance from the curse of sin and eternal
separation from the Father.

I do not want to simplify a story that is not simple; however, a
salvation synopsis on this Christmas Day may be in order.

The Bible is God unveiling Himself to us. It is His story, a present
to unwrap. The central theme of His story is salvation through Jesus
Christ, God's son.

The Old Testament opens with God (see Genesis 1:1). It tells the
saga of the Jewish nation, and prepares the way for the Redeemer. It
communicates the covenant between God and His people through
laws, history, prophecy, and poetry.

The New Testament opens with Christ the Savior (see Matthew 1:1). Then, the history of Christ's church continues with a salvation focus and the second coming of the King.

These pages and words are God-breathed. This saga communicates God's inestimable love for us, as well as our profound need of rescue.

Dear reader, where do you find yourself in this salvation story? You must ask yourself: *Have I acknowledged Jesus as my Savior?* Perhaps time has passed and you have shelved this relationship. Maybe difficulties paved your way for a season, and you blamed God. Have unwise choices created a perceived barrier between you and God?

Wherever you find yourself, He waits for you there. The biggest gift ever given is Jesus, your Savior.

Thanks be to God for His unspeakable gift!
—2 Corinthians 9:15 KJV

Merry Christmas!

Reflection

1. Who do you say He is? See John 10:9 and John 14:6.

2. It's your turn. Share the gift of the Savior with others this Christmas Day.

Prayer

Dear Savior, You were born to save. This is Your season. This is our season, and I savor You this Christmas Day. You are the center of my attention. Thank You for the Bible. Thank You for saving me. It was the best Christmas gift I could ever receive.

Amen

Good Christian Men, Rejoice

John Mason Neale, Nineteenth Century
[Verses 1 and 3]

Good Christian men, rejoice

With heart and

soul and voice;

Give ye heed to what we say:

Jesus Christ was born today.

Ox and ass before him bow,

And he is in the manger now.

Christ is born today!

Christ is born today!

Good Christian men, rejoice

With heart and soul and voice;

Now ye need not fear the grave:

Jesus Christ was born to save!

Calls you one and calls you all

To gain his everlasting hall

Christ was born to save!

Christ was born to save!

Gratitude spills over. First, I thank my Savior. The purpose of my life is to know You, make You known, and encourage others along the way. Thank You for loving and leading me here.

Next, my family and friends (my tribe). Thank you for cheering me on and for your excitement about this project. To my husband Dan, for editorial and technical support. For telling me (multiple times) that I was not crazy (I have since learned that most authors feel crazy at some point while writing a book), when I was emphatic that I was indeed crazy. This book would not have happened without you. To my precious sons, Samuel, Noah, Josiah, and Micah, you lifted me with your interest and eagerness about this venture.

Thank you, Michael Johnson, for your input. I am forever grateful. To the readers of my Purposeful Encouragement blog, thank you for reading my words. You inspire me with your comments, messages, vulnerability, and support. Because you read, I write.

Finally, dear reader, I thank you for jumping on this Advent expedition with me.

For more connection, look for me here:

www.kristinsaatzer.com

@kmysaatzer

Facebook.com/ENCOURAGEONPURPOSE

Order Information

To order additional copies of this book, please visit
www.redemption-press.com.
Also available on Amazon.com and BarnesandNoble.com
Or by calling toll-free 1-844-2REDEEM.